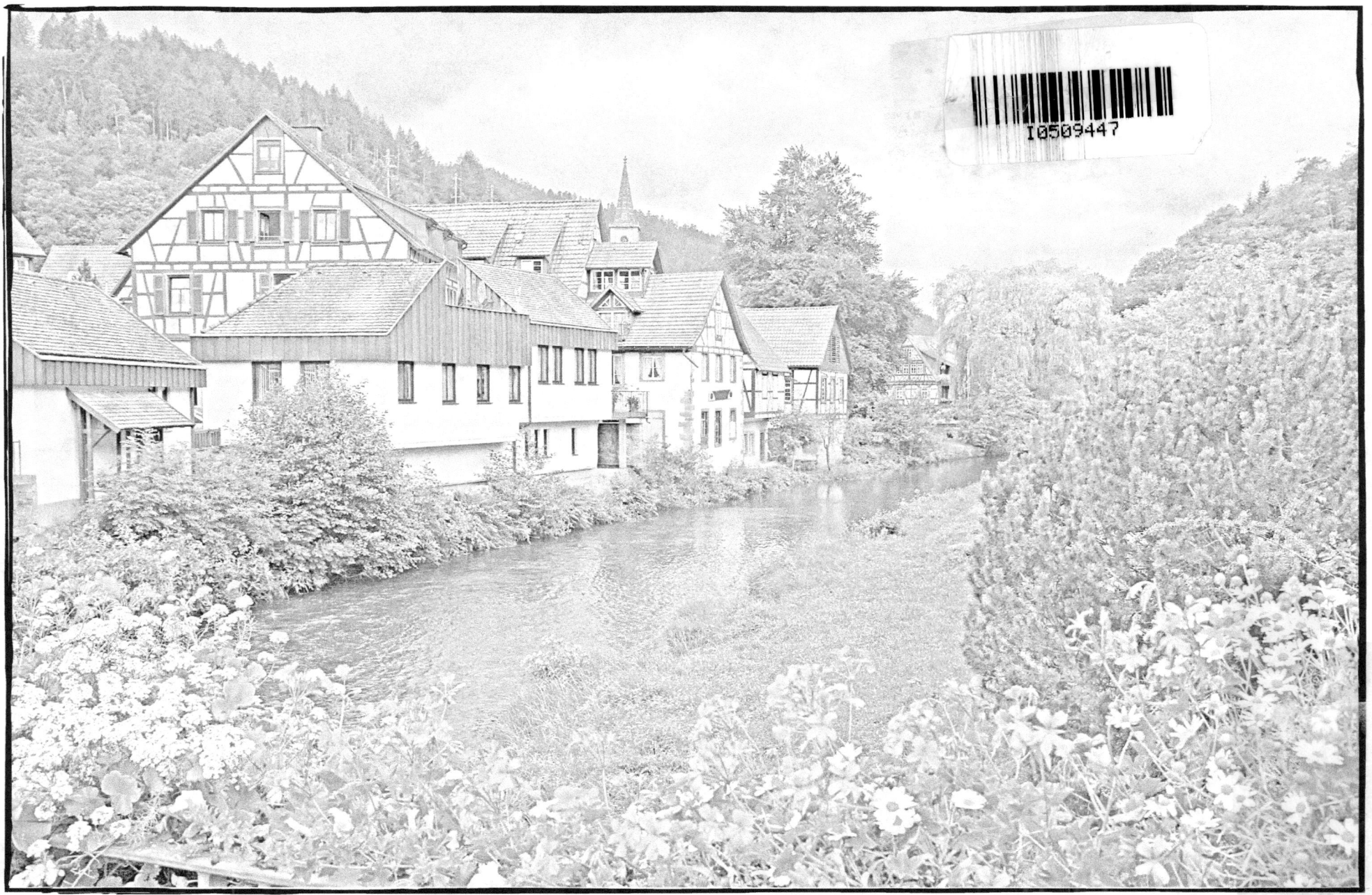

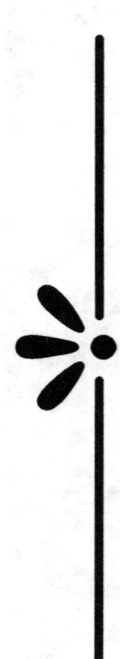

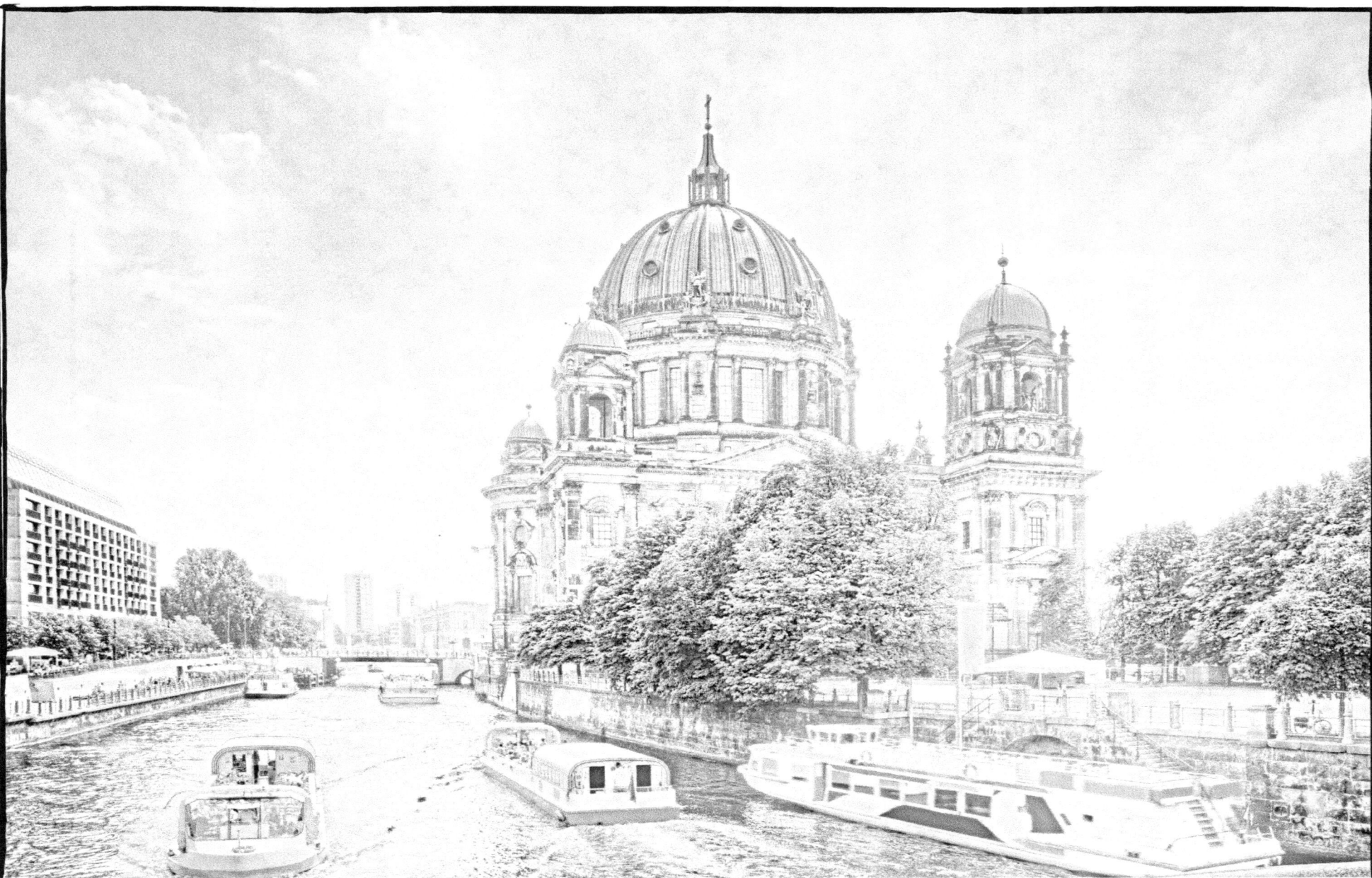

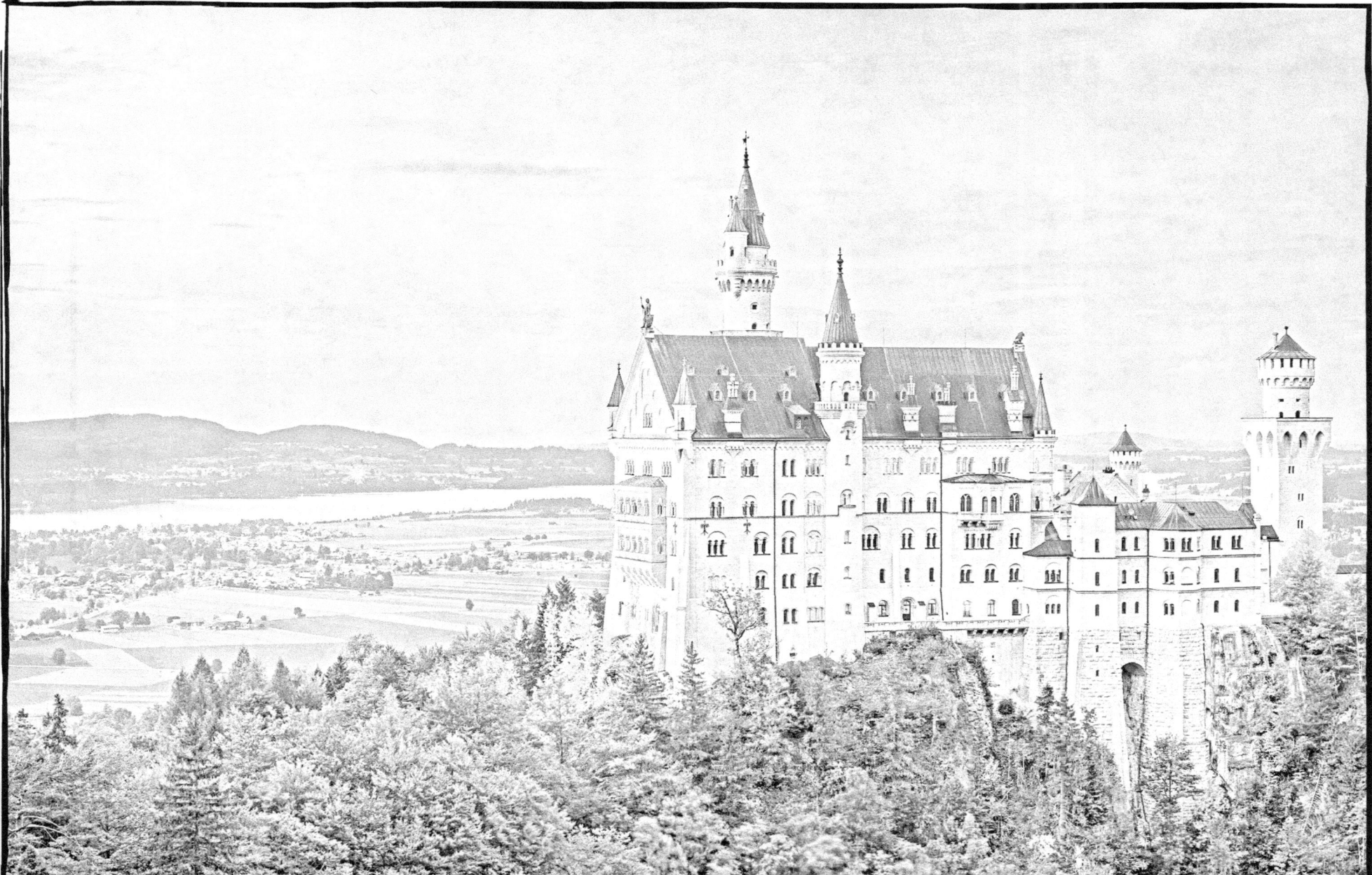

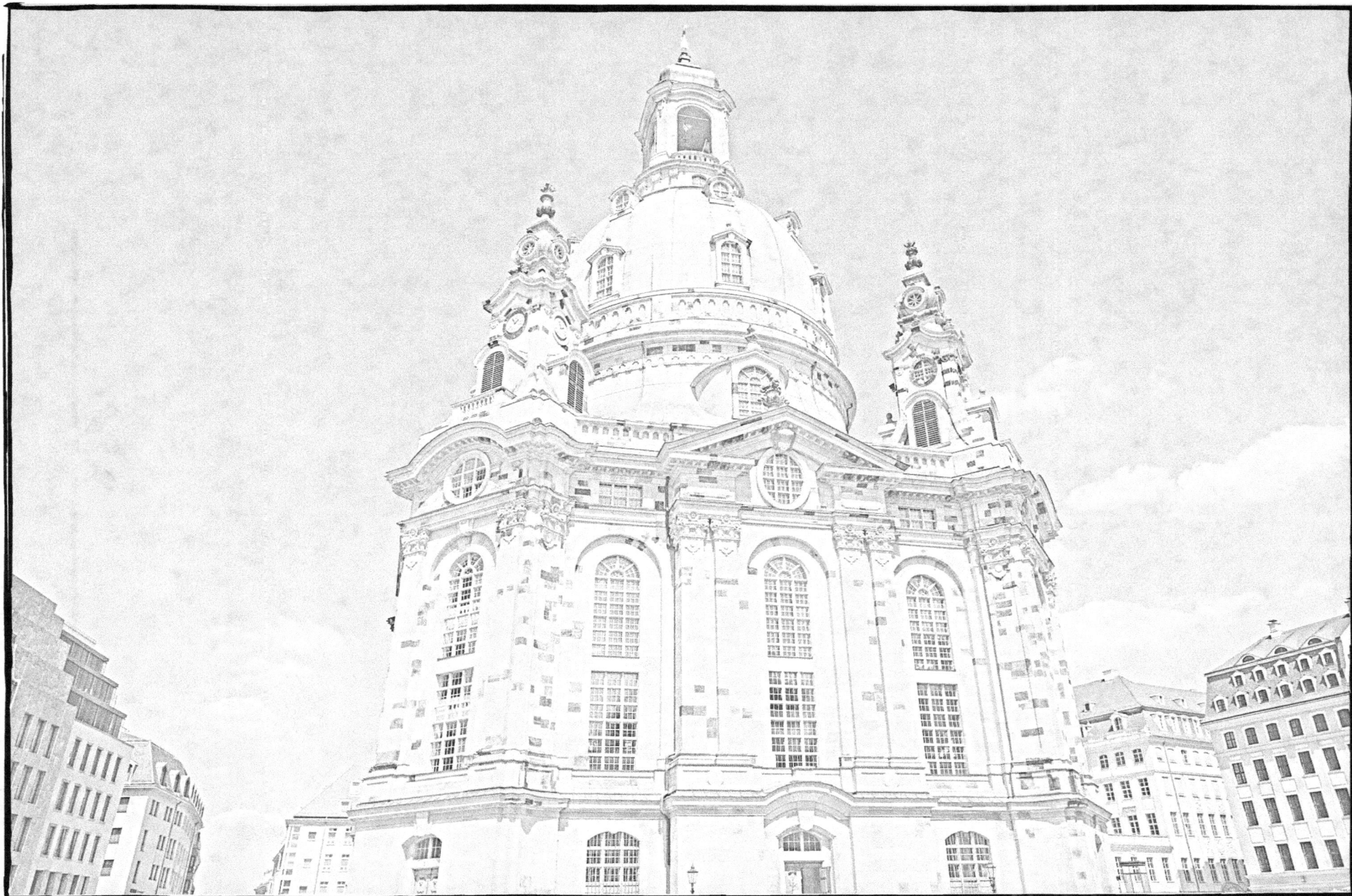

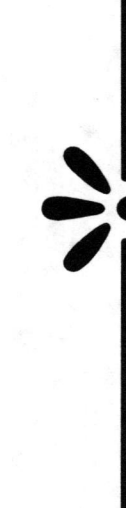

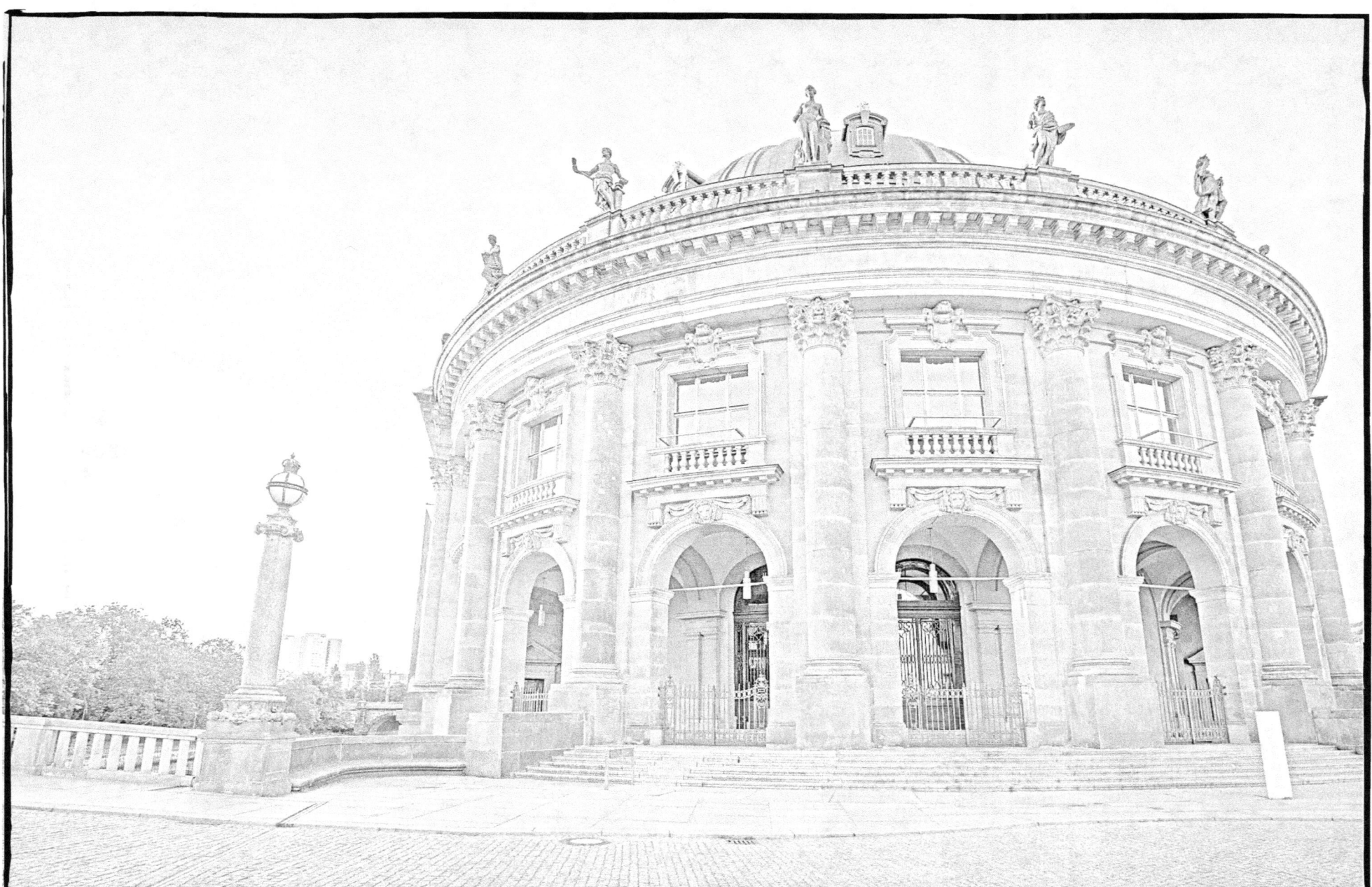

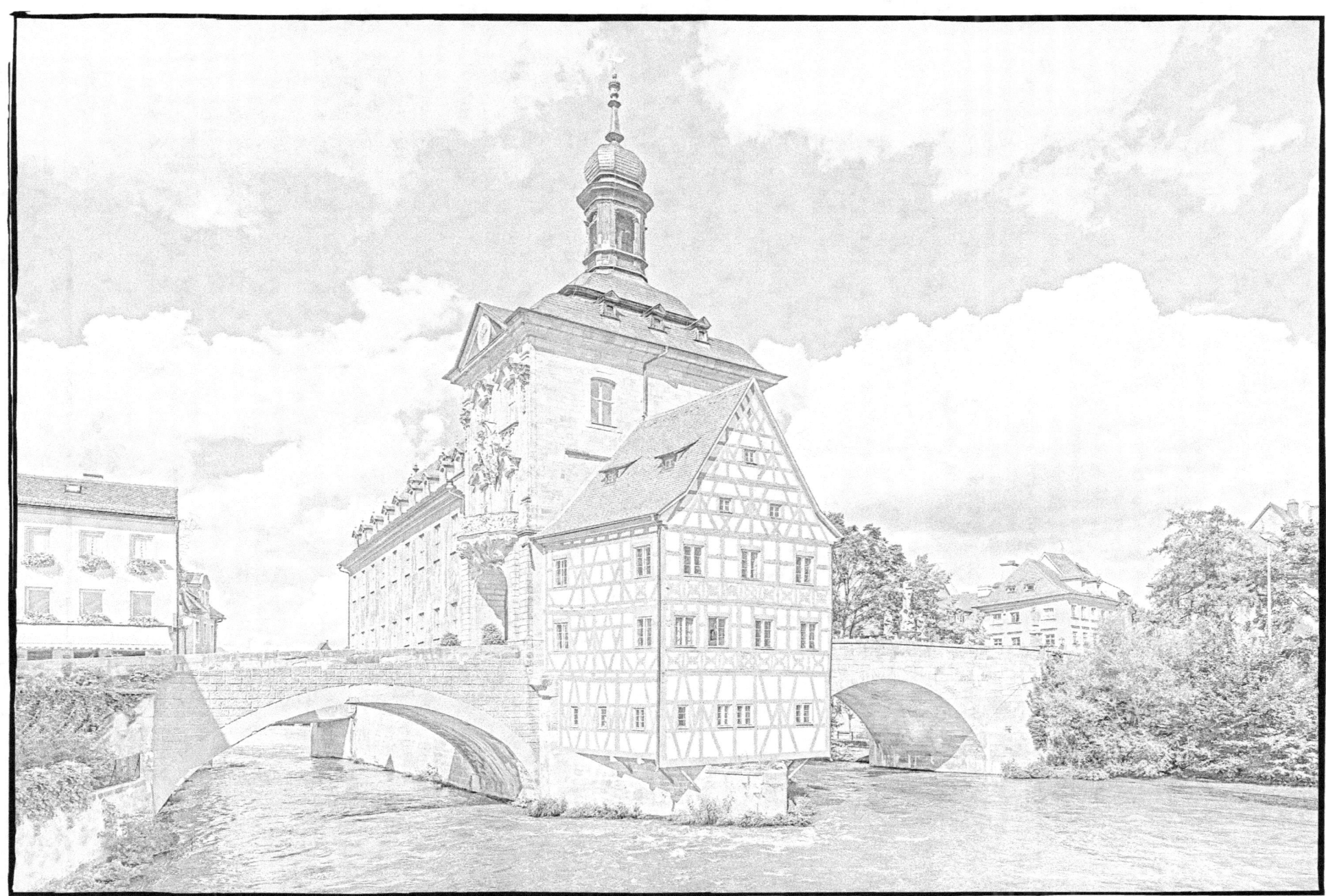

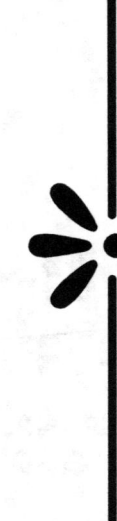

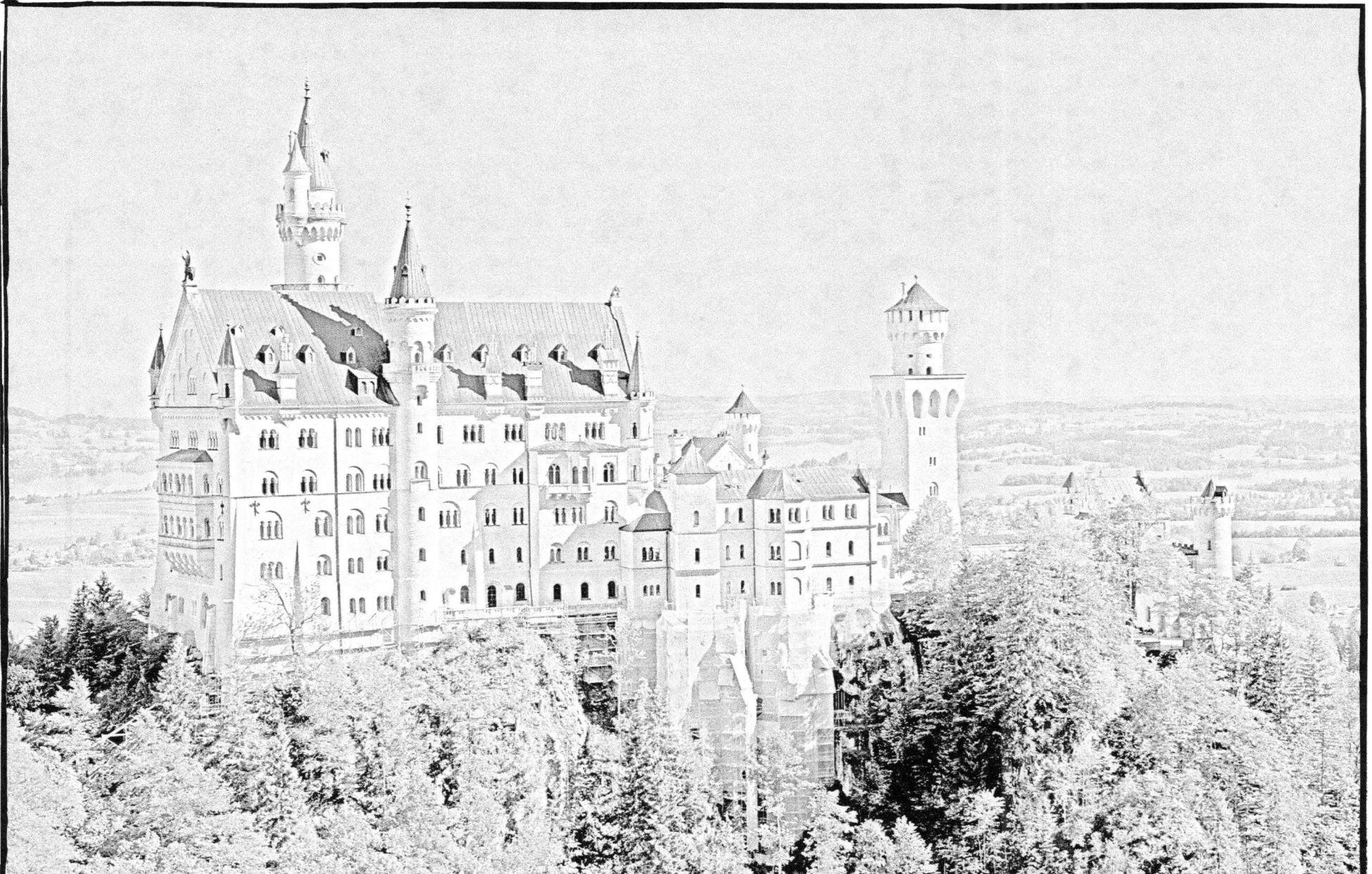

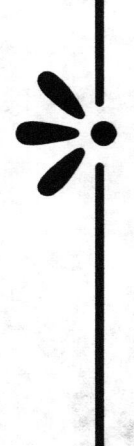

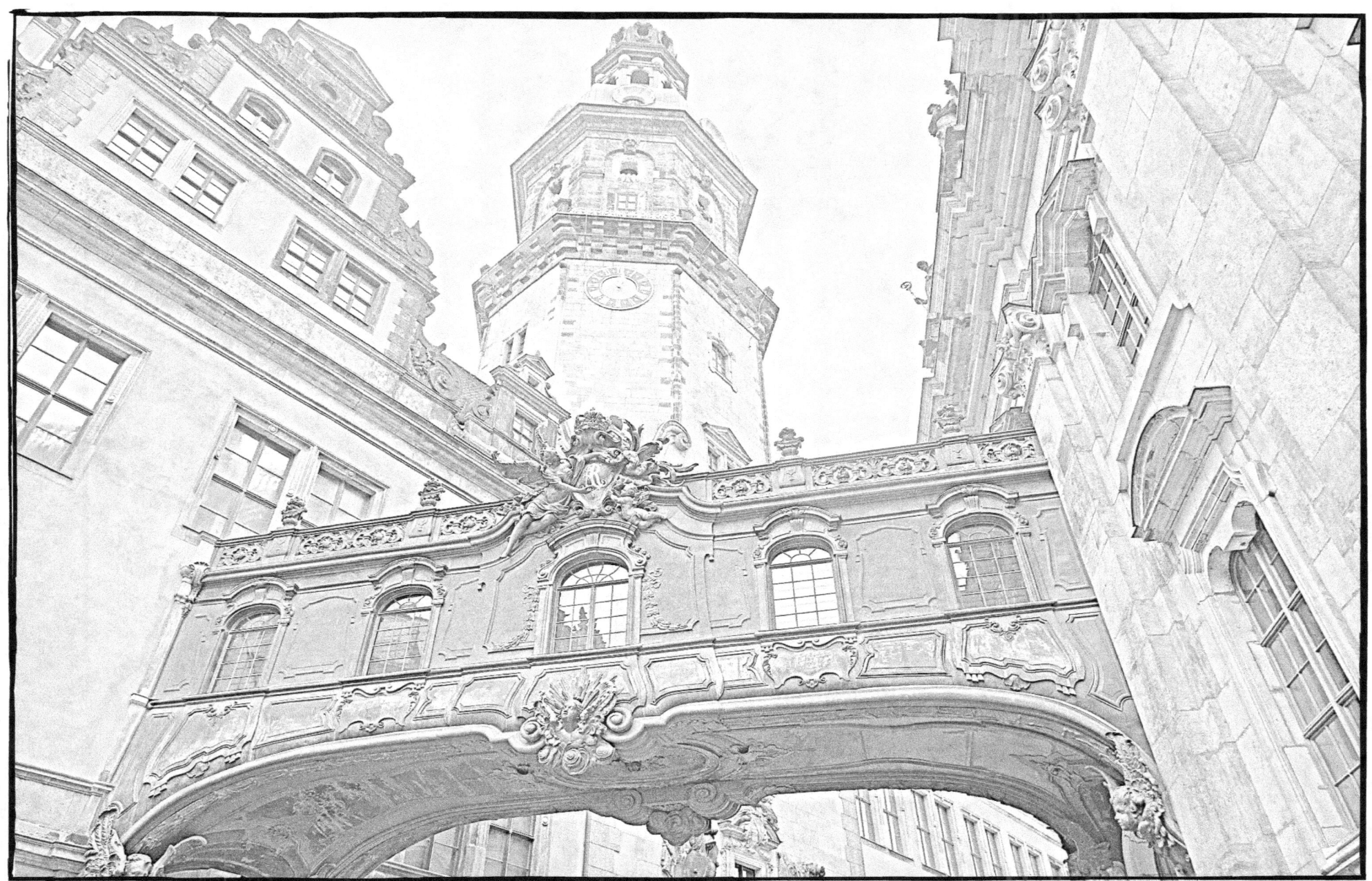

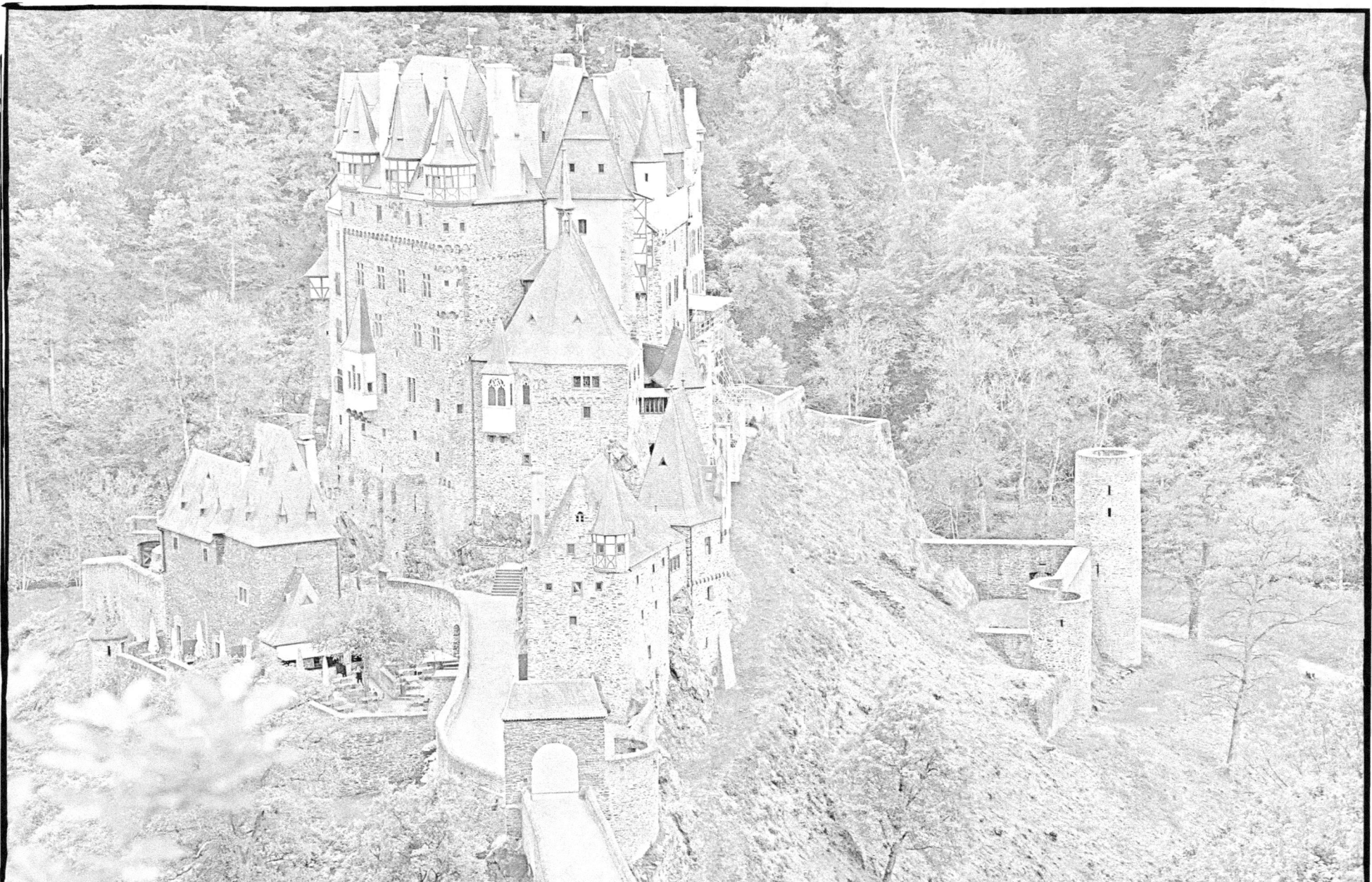

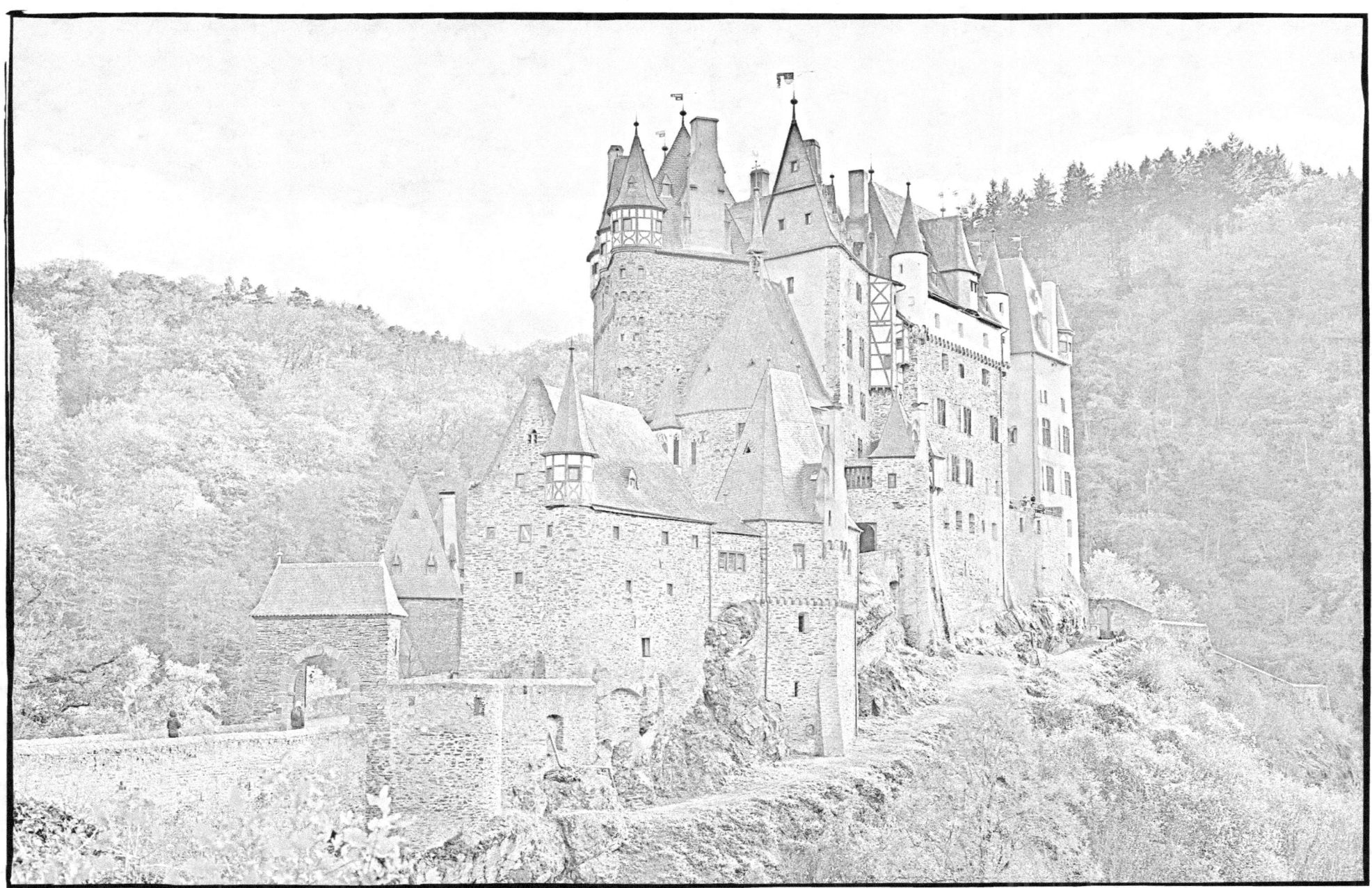

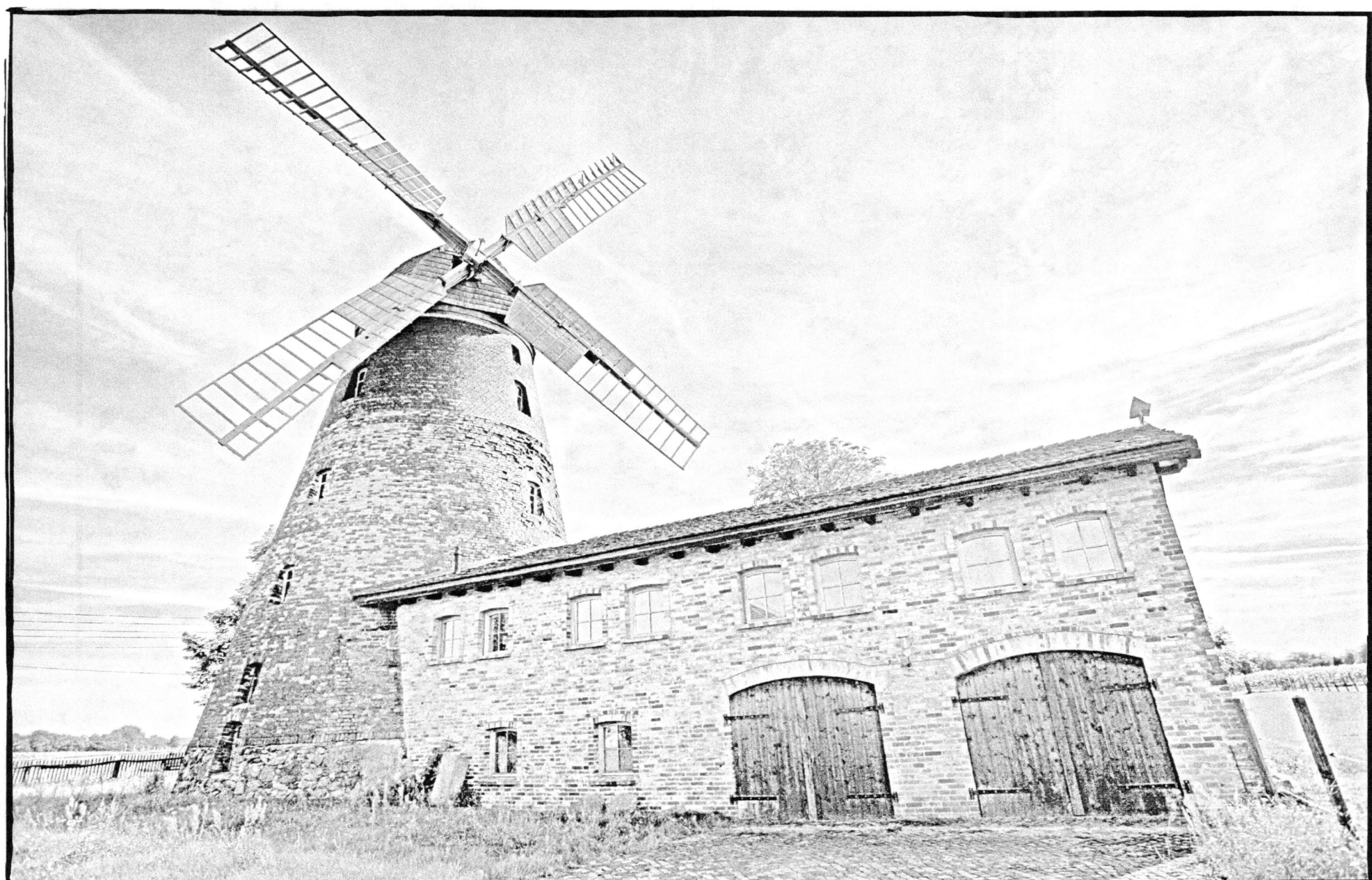

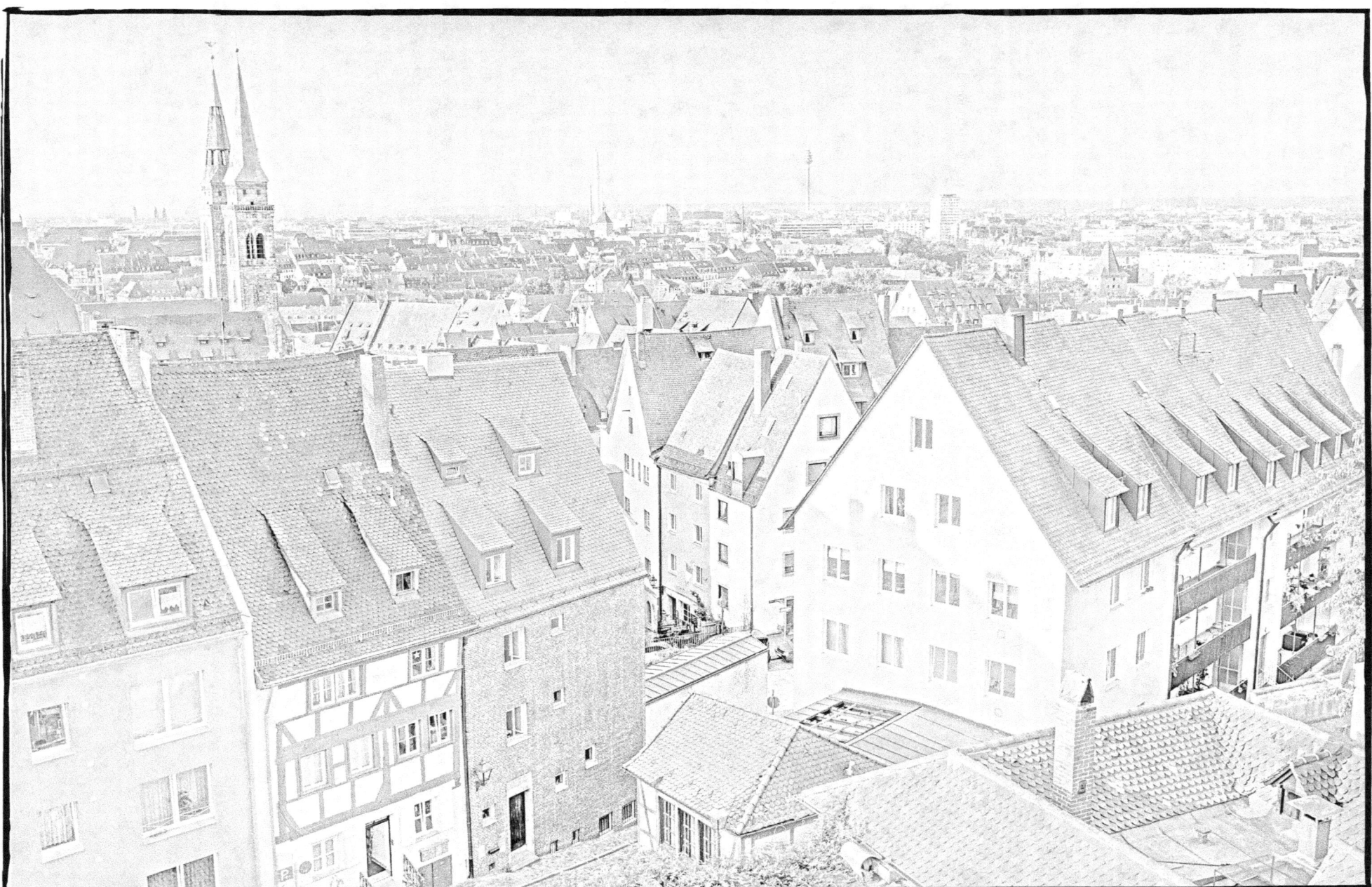

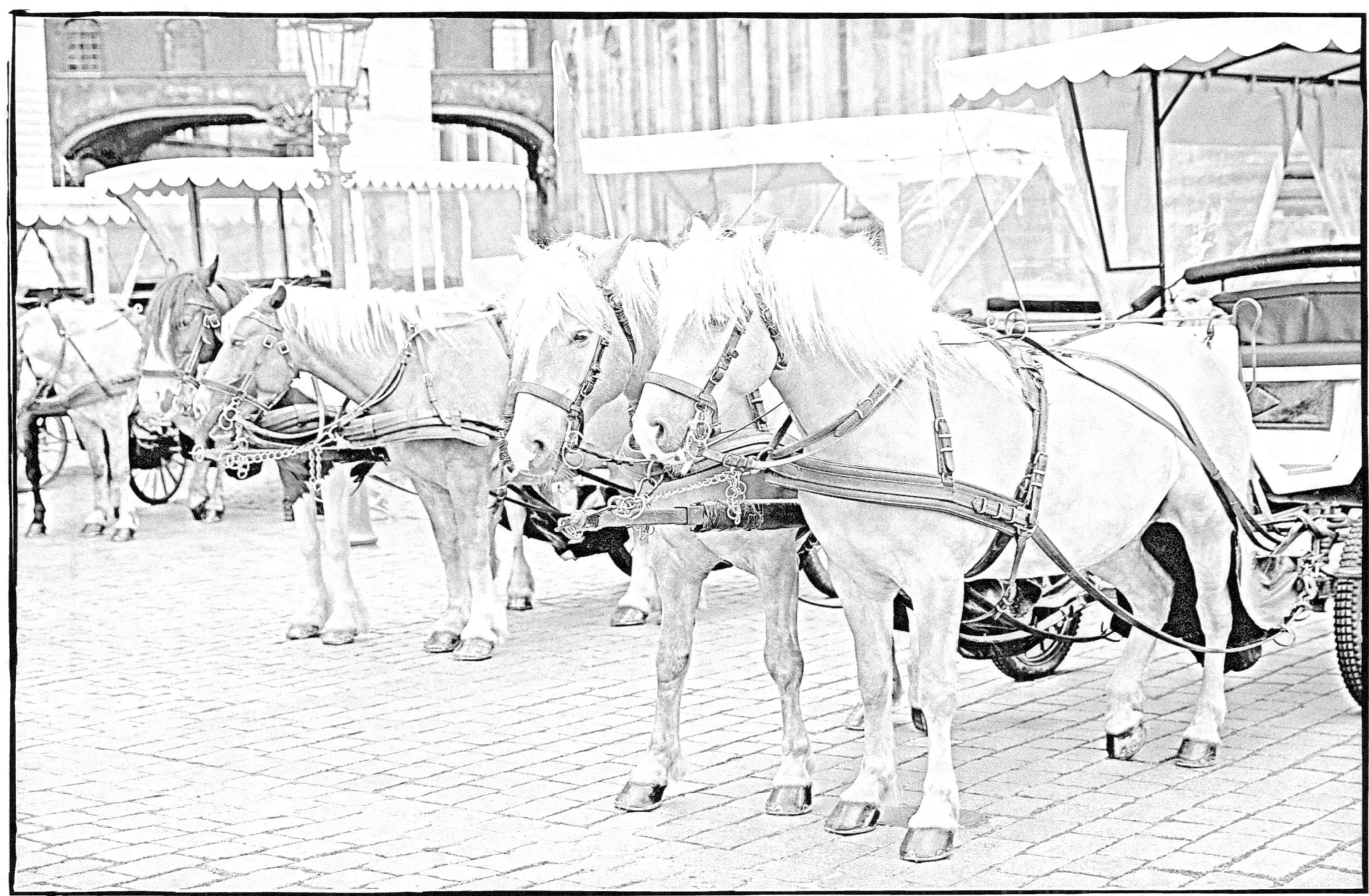

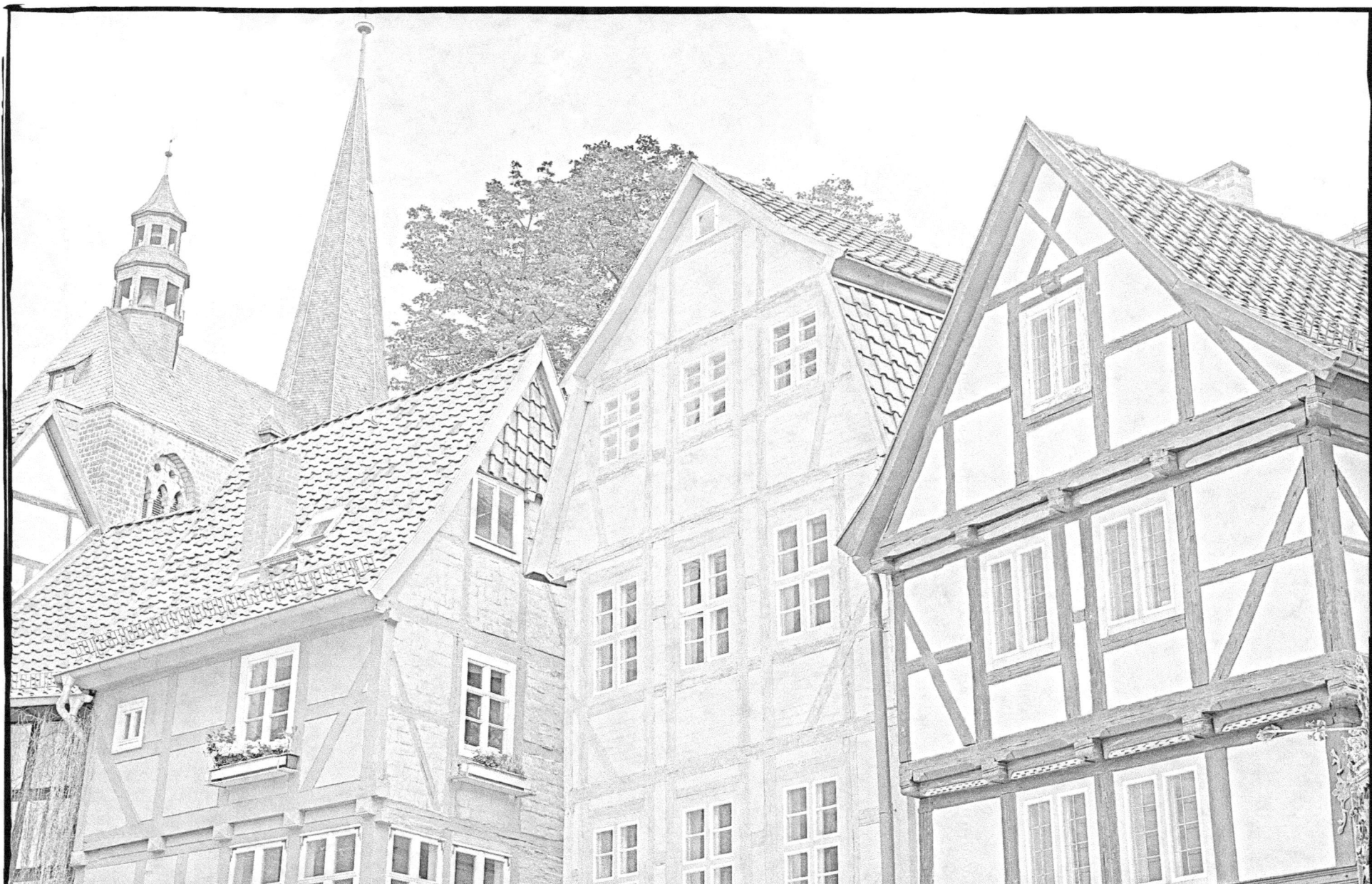

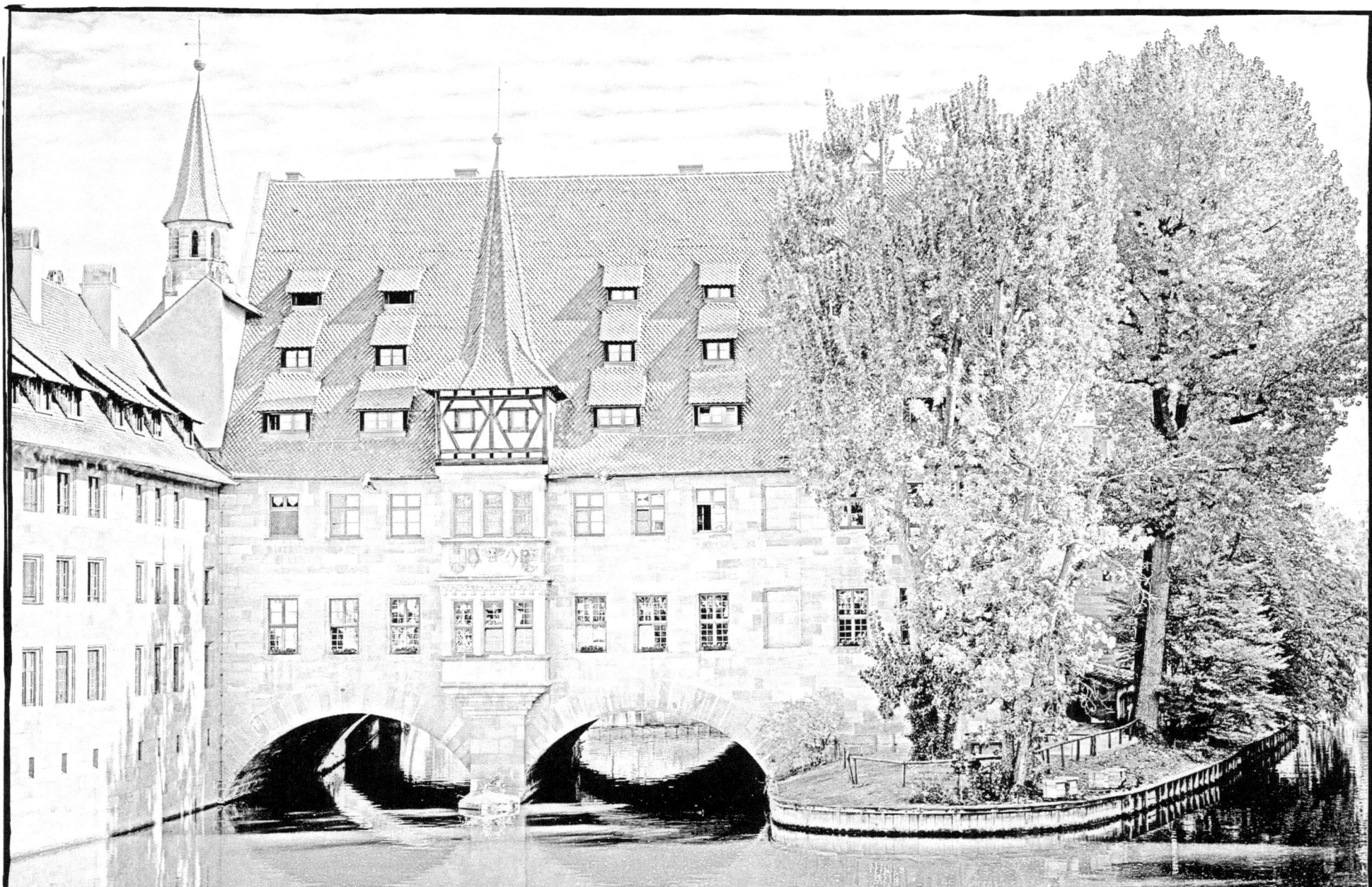

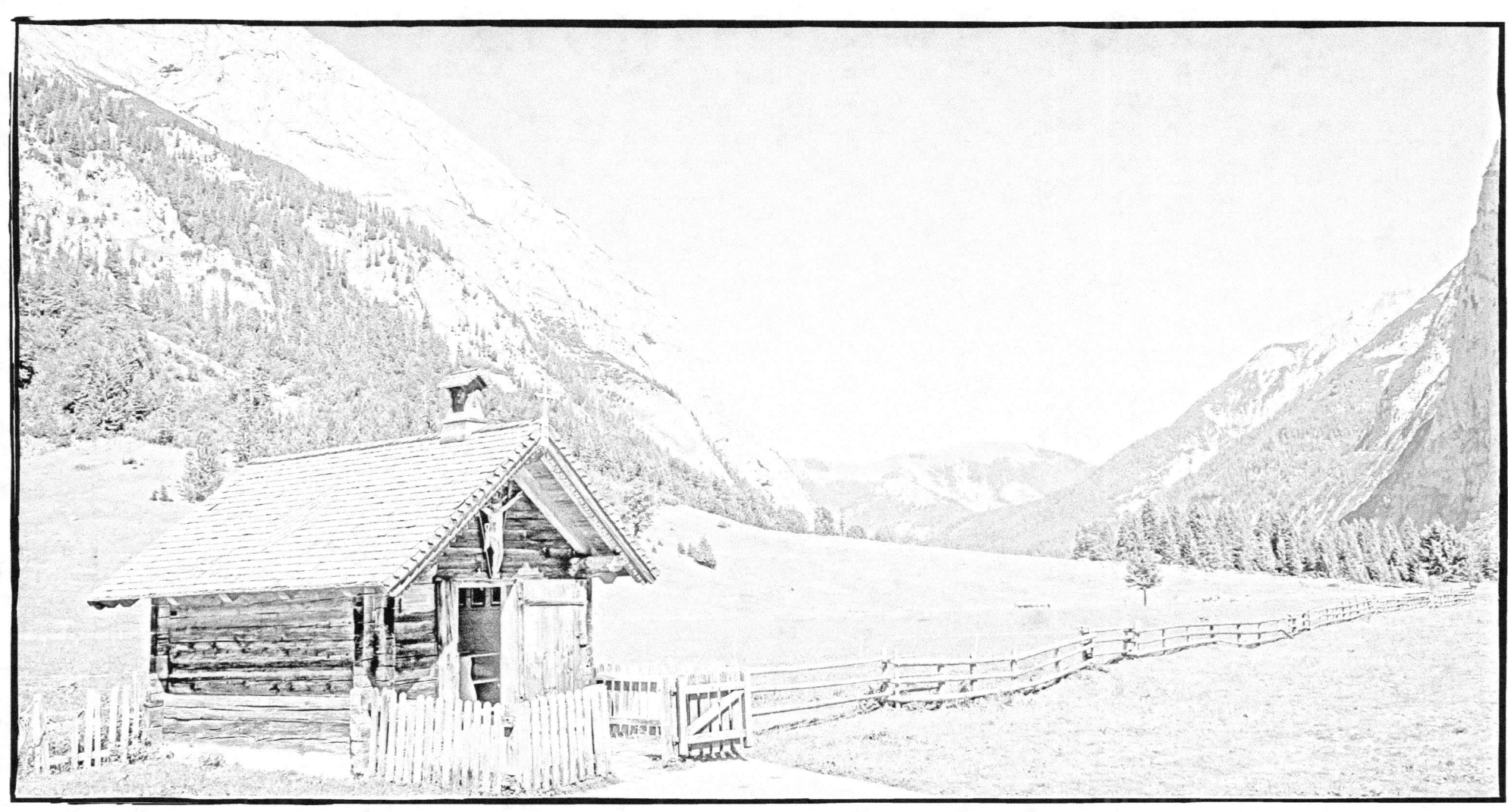

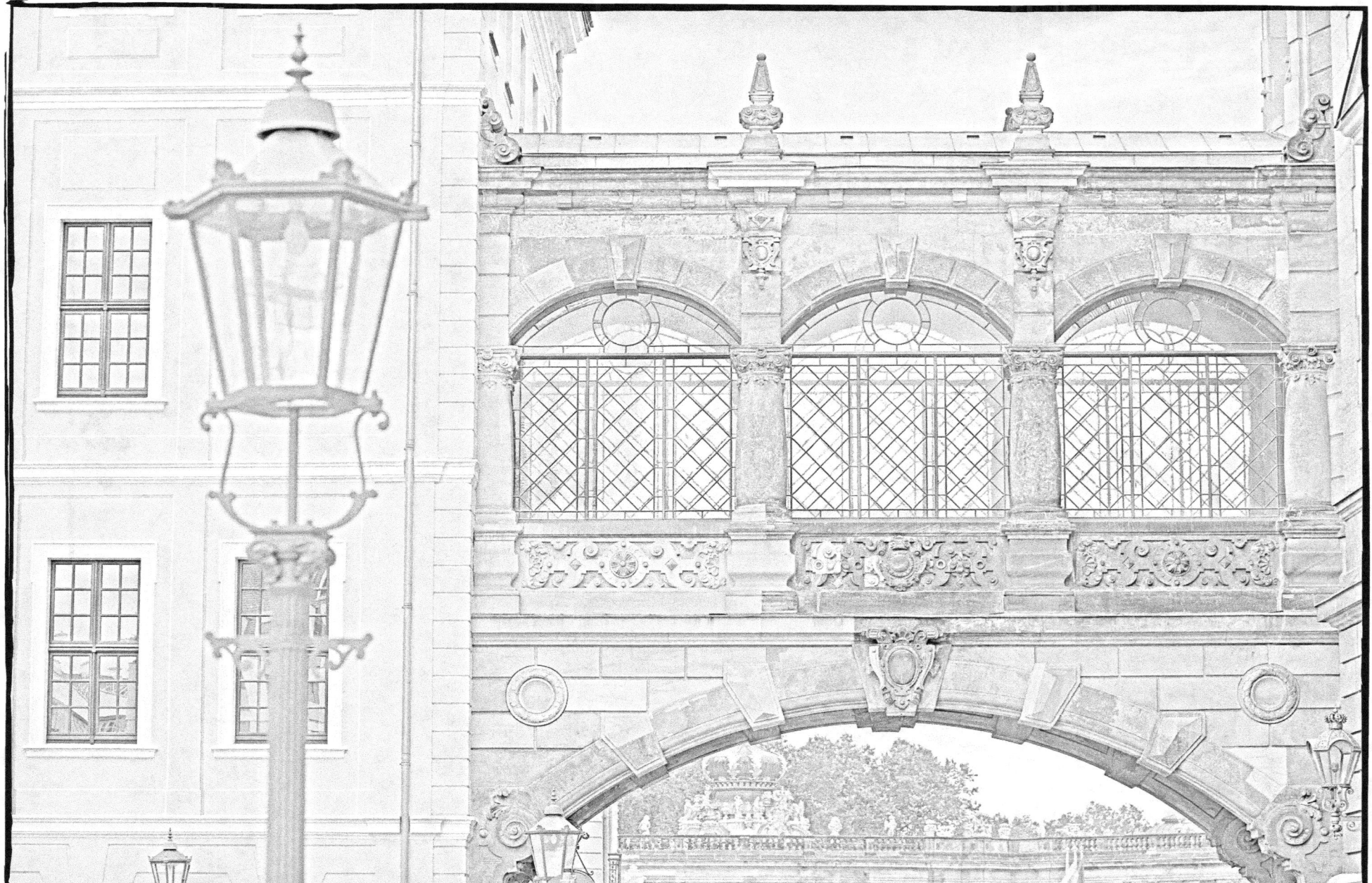

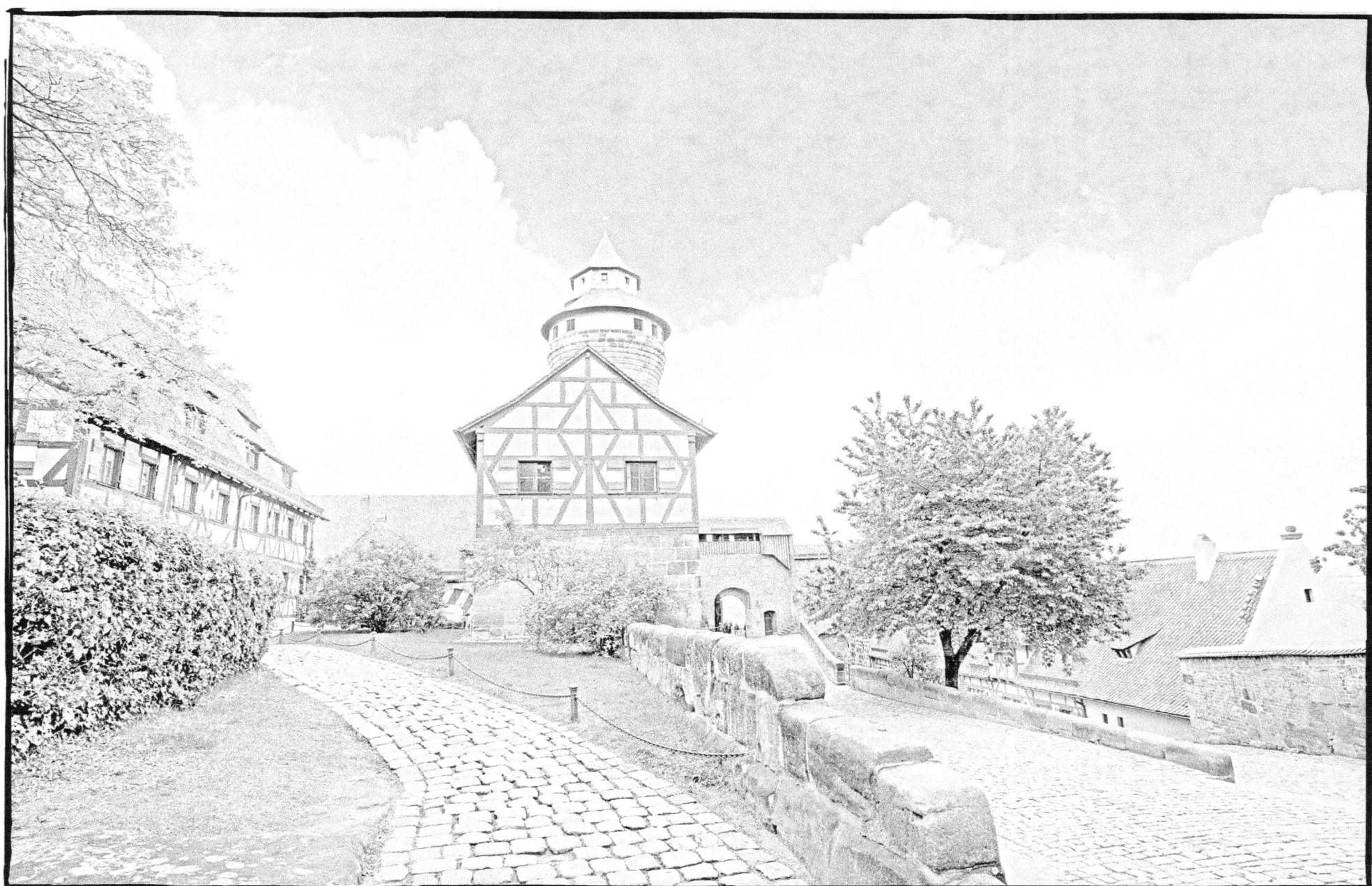

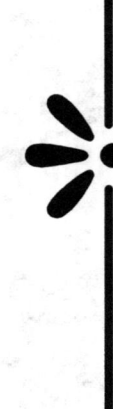

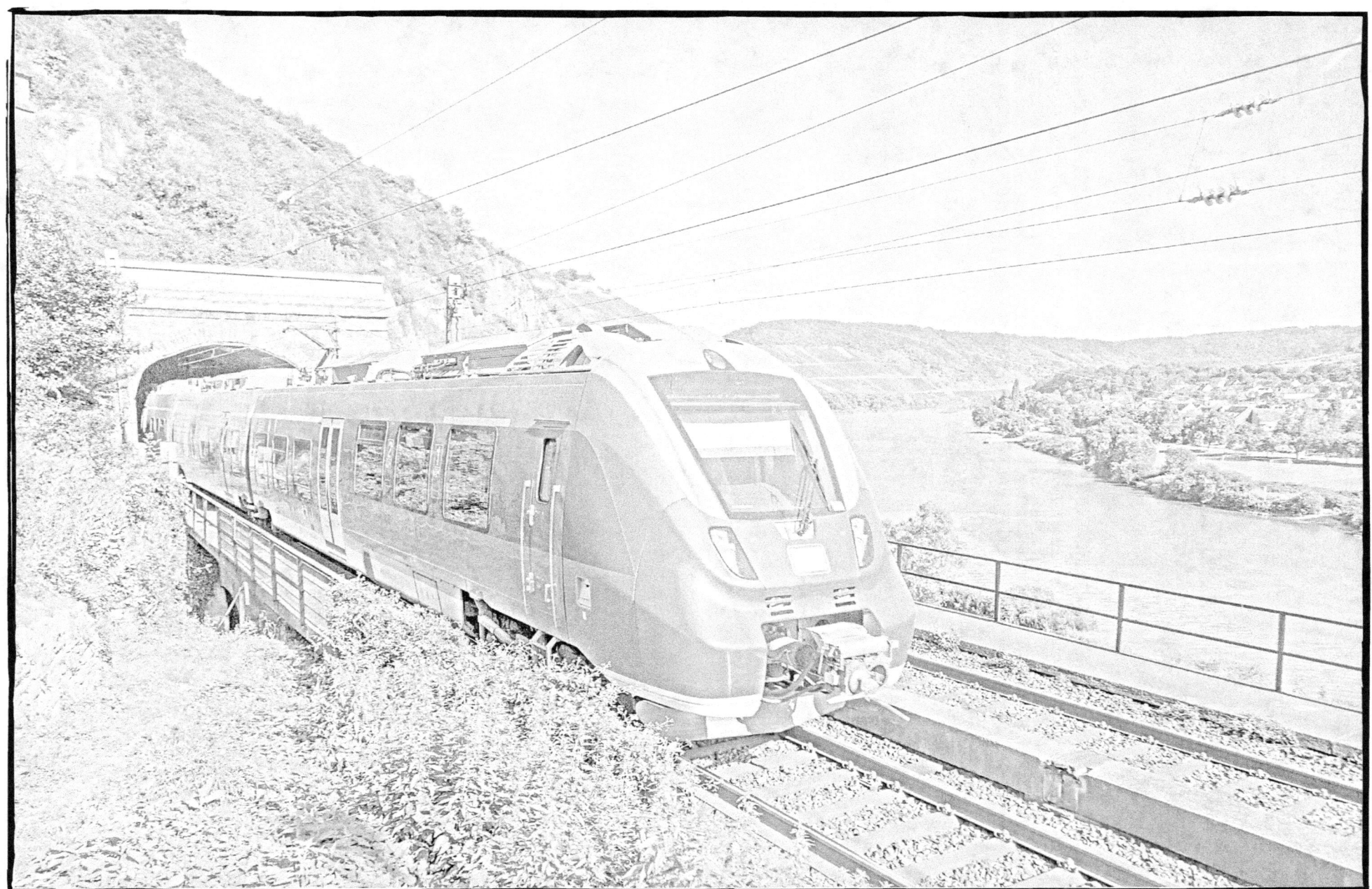

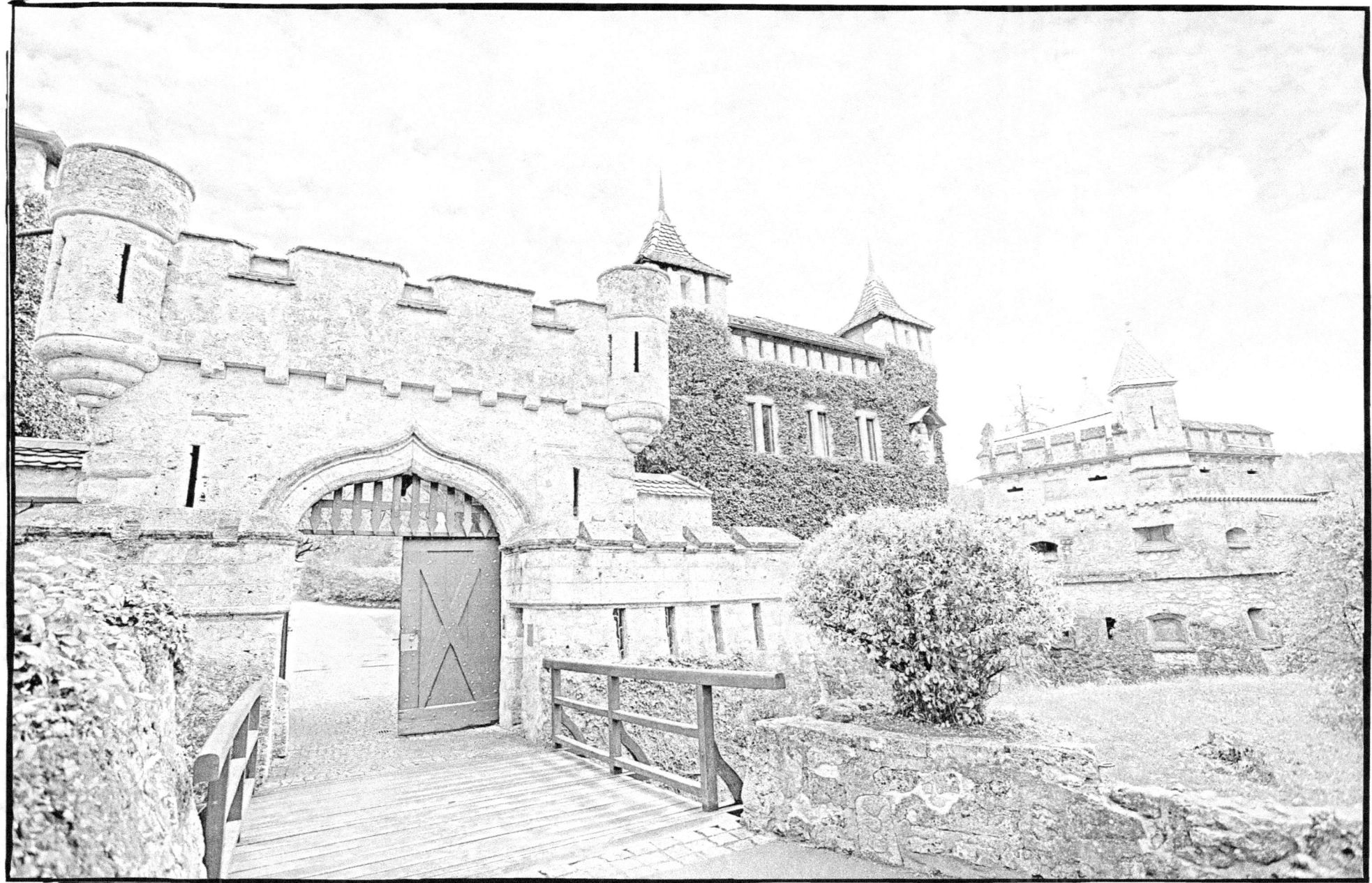

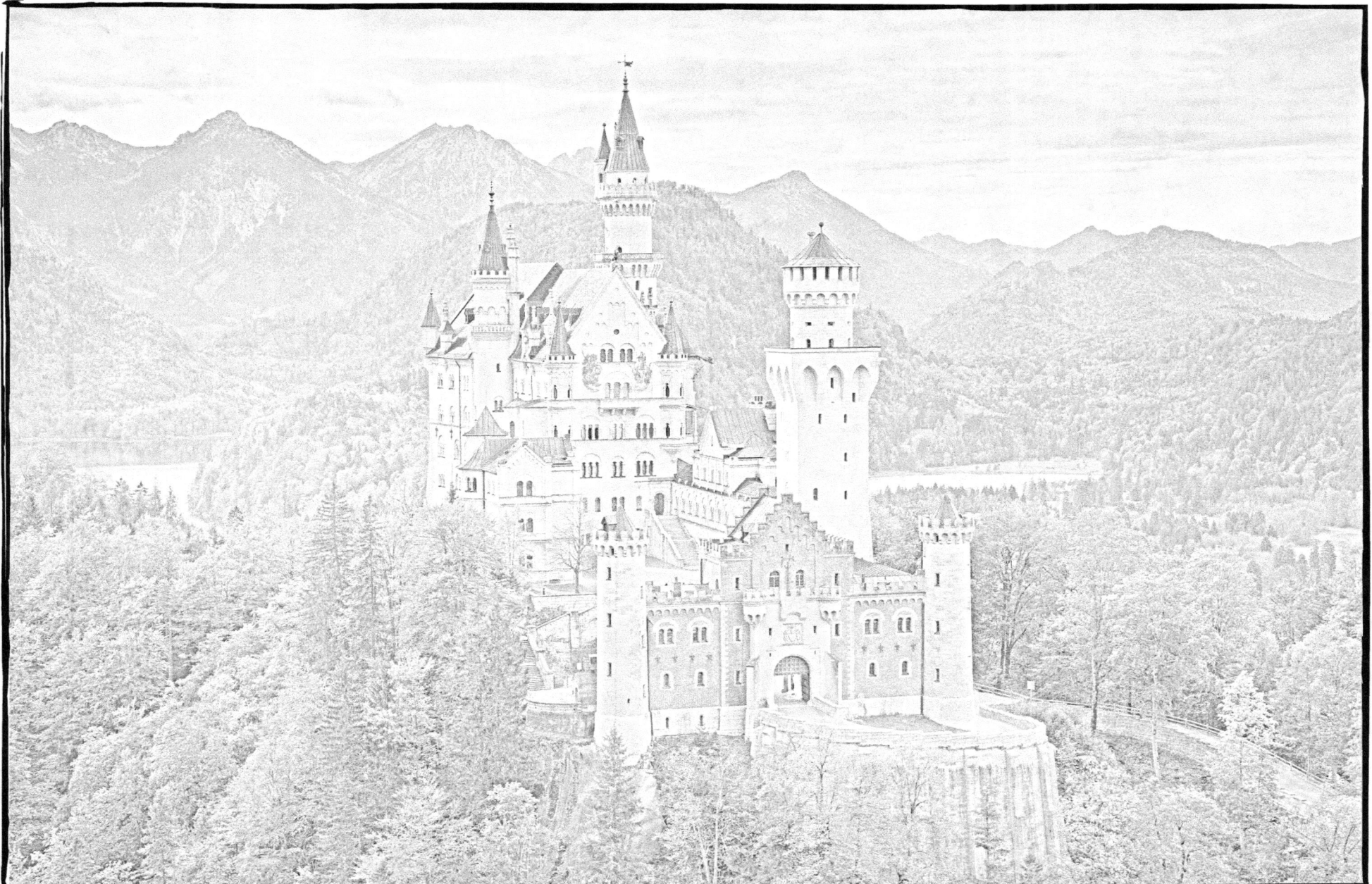

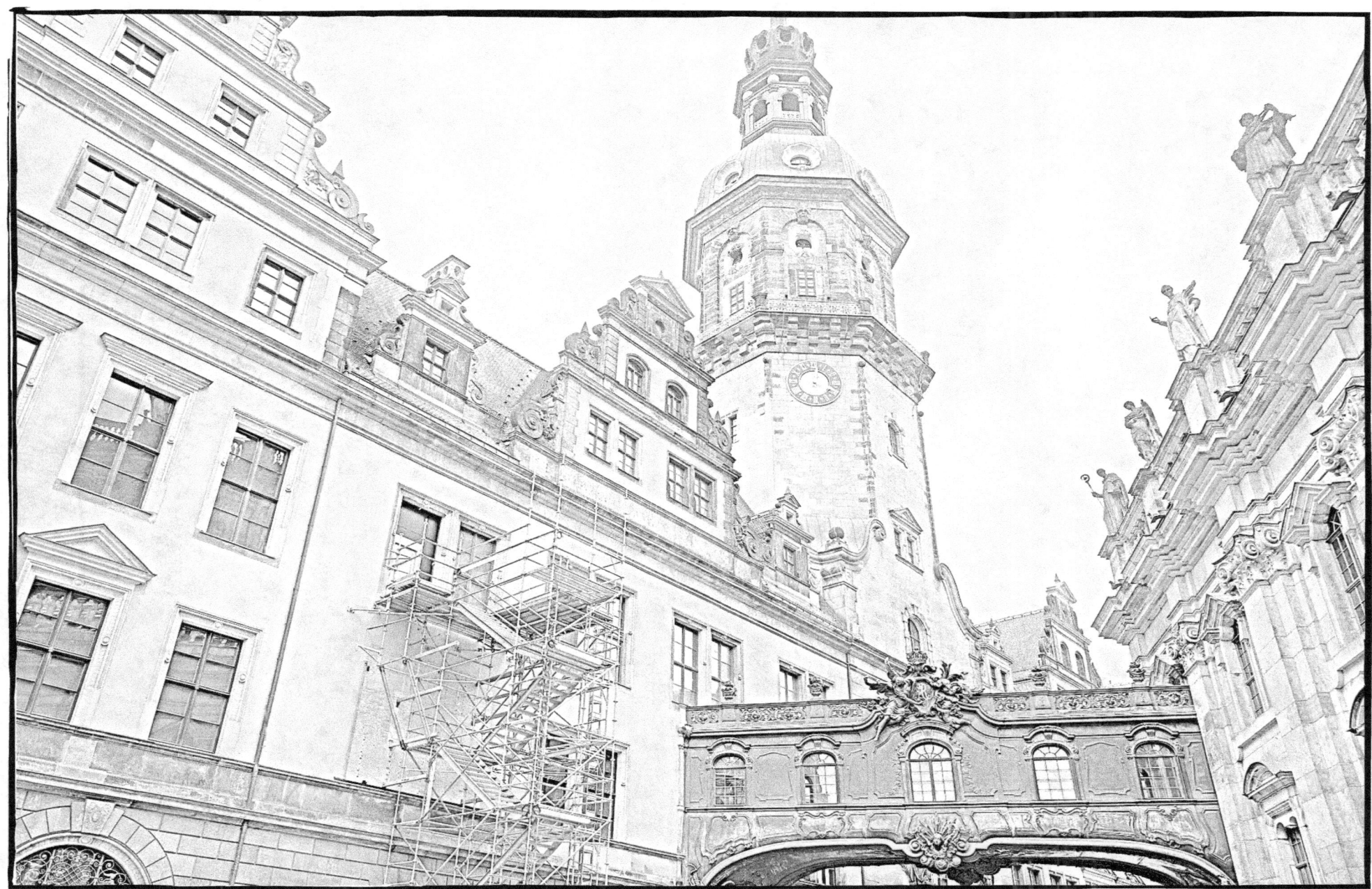

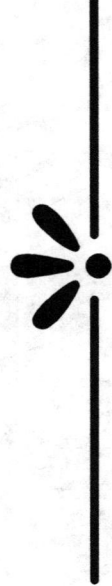

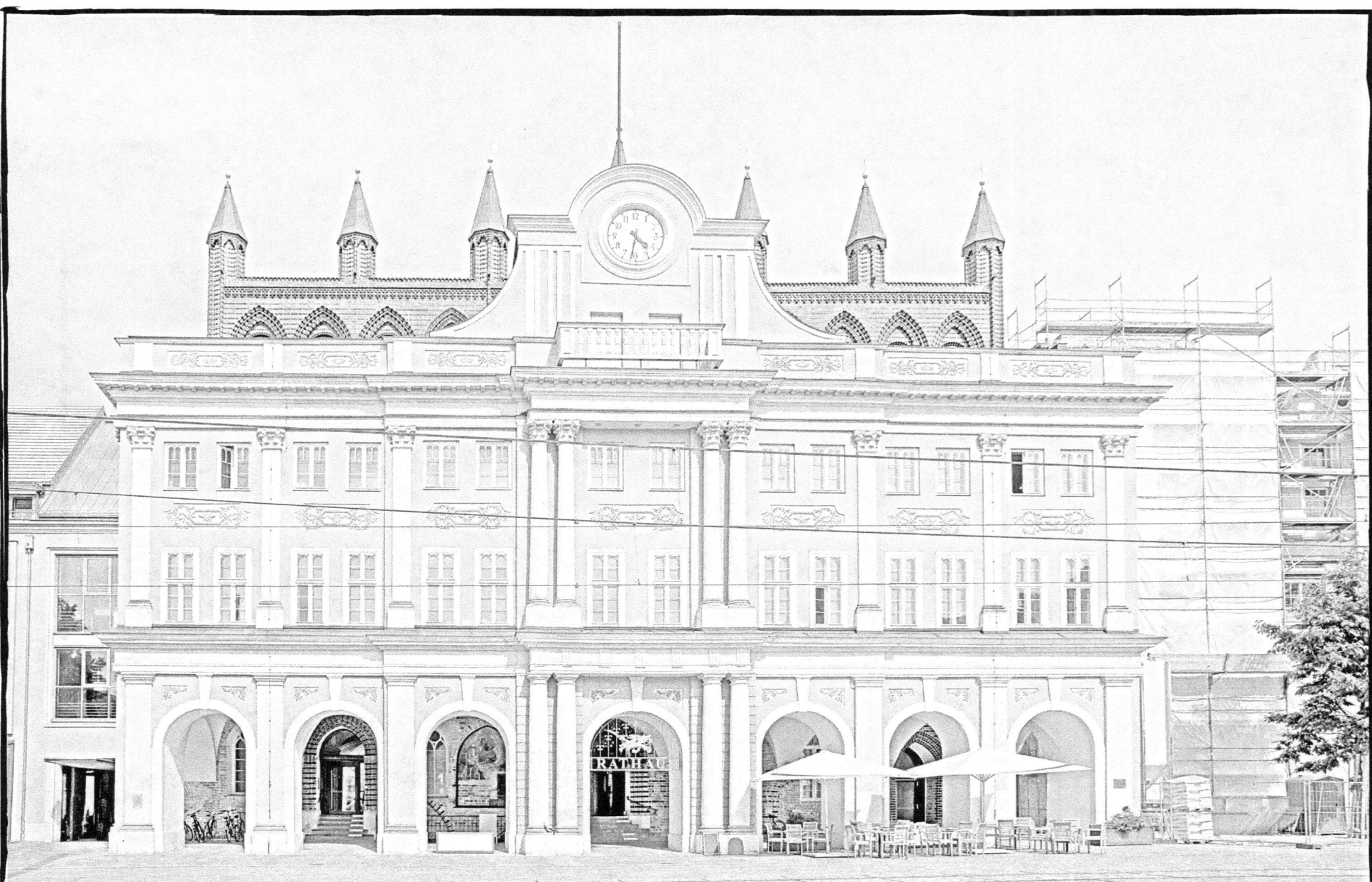

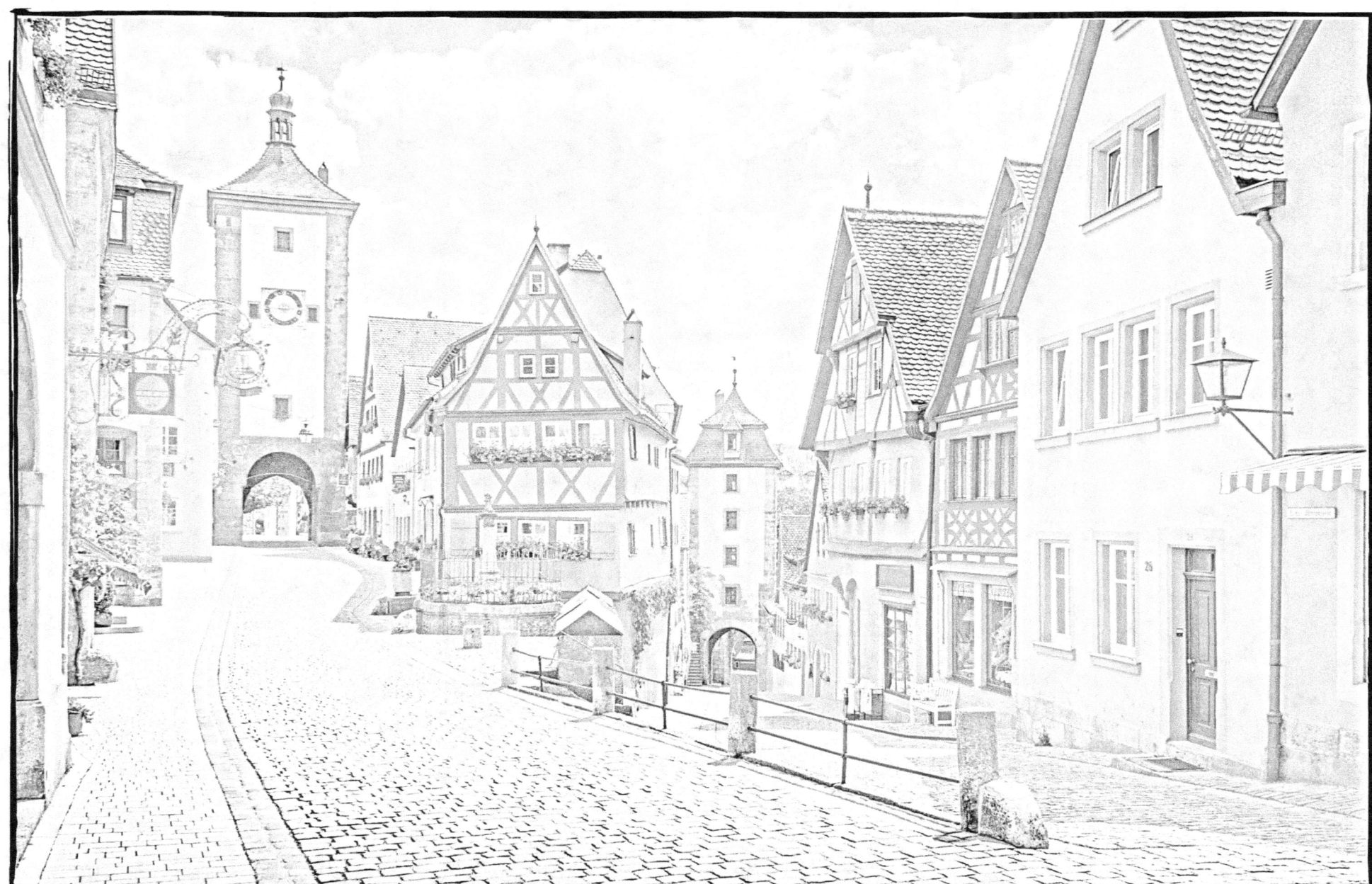

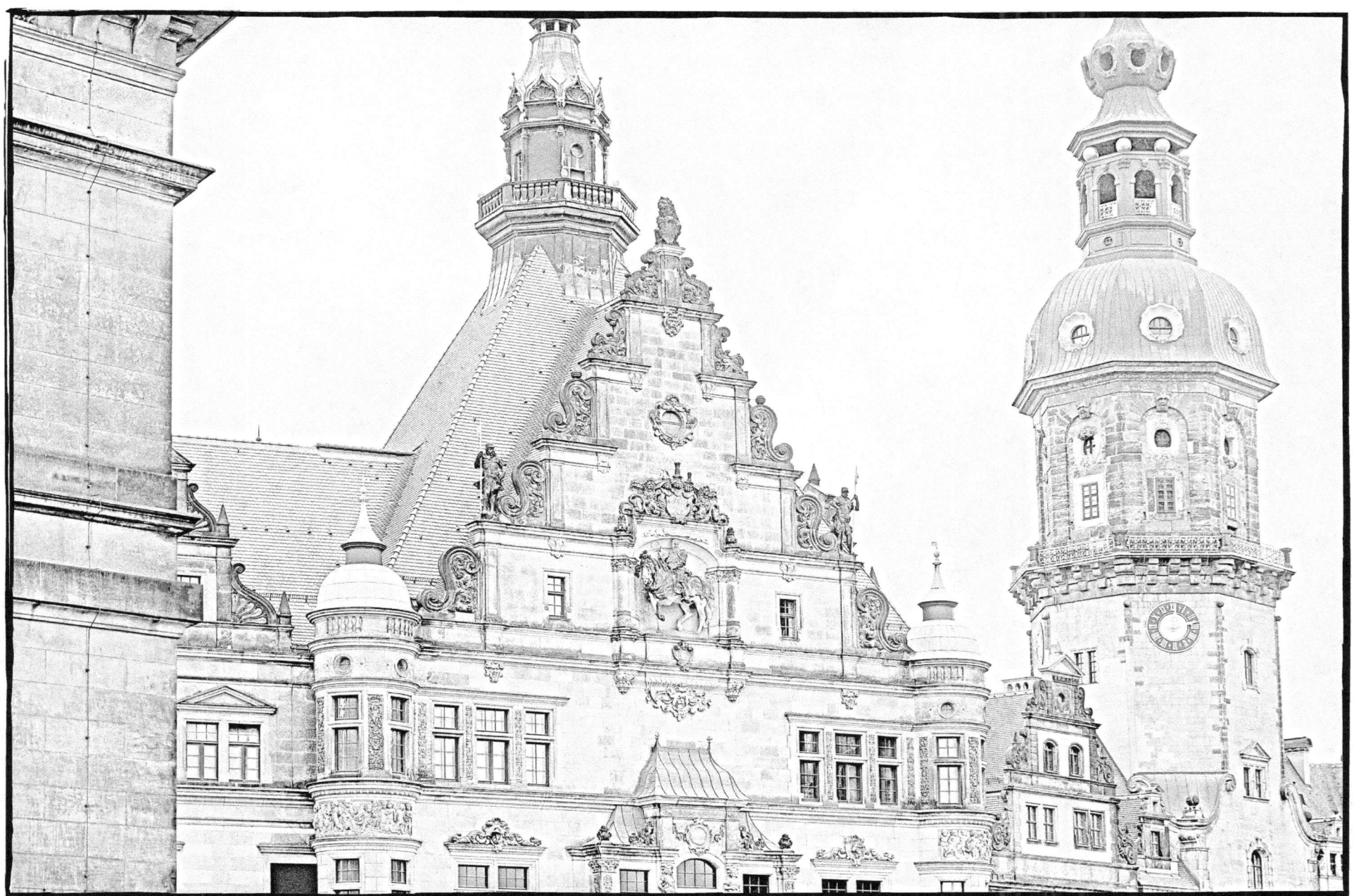

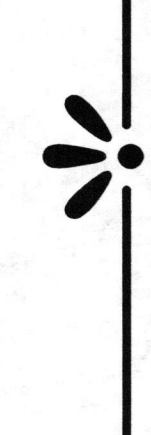

Germany Grayscale Coloring Book

Copyright © 2020 by A. Kamci

All rights reserved.
No part of this book may be reproduced without written permission of the copyright owner, except for the use of limited quotations for the purpose of book reviews.